C0062 02121

D0676148

# Guess Who's in Grass

**Picture credits**
(t=top, b=bottom, l=left, r=right, c=centre, fc=front cover)
**FLPA:** 4–5, 12–13 Richard Du Toit/Minden Pictures; 6–7 Roger Tidman; 8–9 Winfried Wisniewski/FN/
Minden; 10–11 Pete Oxford/Minden Pictures; 14–15 Richard Becker
**Shutterstock:** fc Simon_g; 3 Anan Kaewkhammul; 16–17 Eric Isselee; 18–19 Jackiso

GLASGOW LIFE GLASGOW LIBRARIES

C006202121

WITHDRAWN

| G | PETERS |
| 26-Jan-2015 | £5.99 |
| J591.74 | |

Editor: Ruth Symons
Cover Designer: Krina Patel
Editorial Director: Victoria Garrard
Art Director: Laura Roberts-Jensen

Copyright © QED Publishing 2014

First published in the UK in 2014 by
QED Publishing, a Quarto Group company
The Old Brewery, 6 Blundell Street
London N7 9BH

www.qed-publishing.co.uk

All rights reserved. No part of this publication may be reproduced, stored
in a retrieval system, or transmitted in any form or by any means, electronic,
mechanical, photocopying, recording, or otherwise, without the prior permission
of the publisher, nor be otherwise circulated in any form of binding or cover other
than that in which it is published and without a similar condition being imposed on
the subsequent purchaser.

A catalogue record for this book is available from the British Library.

ISBN 978 1 78171 537 6

Printed in China

# Guess Who's in the Grass

**Camilla De La Bédoyère and Fiona Hajée**

QED Publishing

Who has black and white stripes?

# I do!
I am a zebra.

I am a foal. When I stand with
other zebras, my stripes make
it hard for lions to see me.

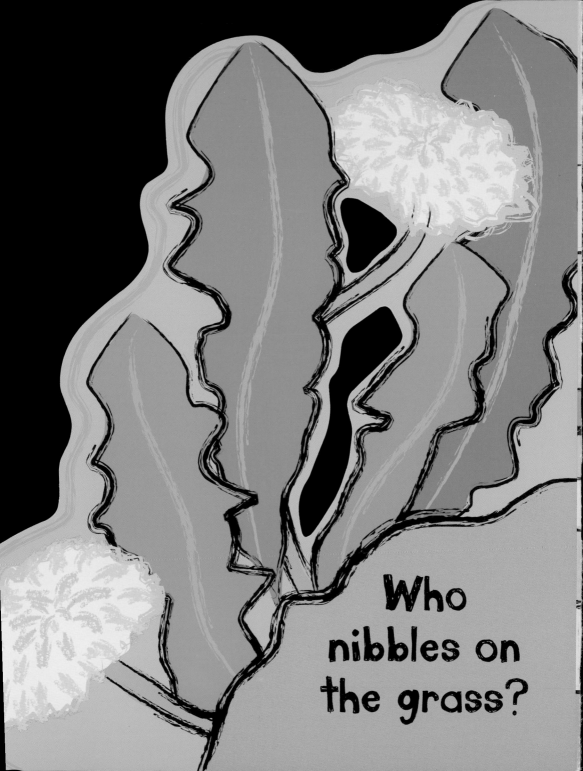

Who
nibbles on
the grass?

I do!
I am a
rabbit.

I always stay close to my underground home - that way I can run to safety if I see a scary animal.

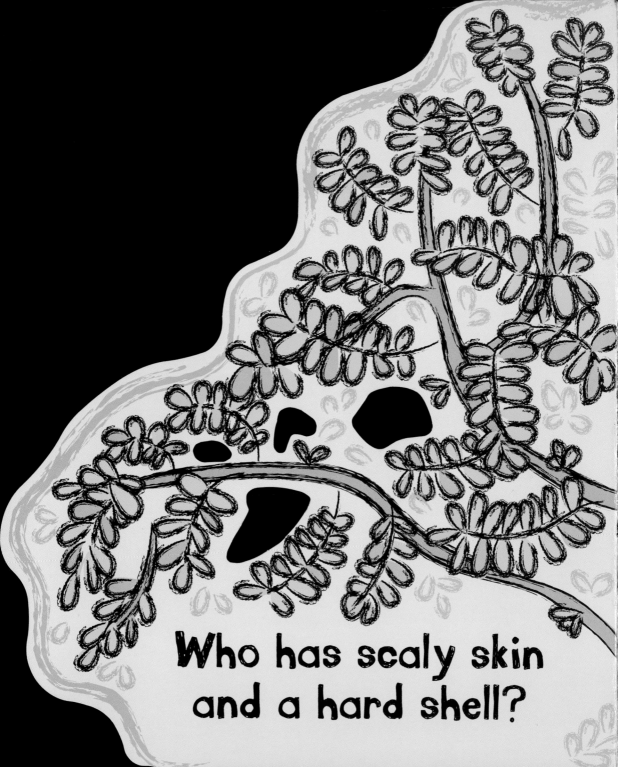

Who has scaly skin
and a hard shell?

Lions want to eat me,
but they can't bite
through my shell!

I do!
I am a
tortoise.

Who has thick, shaggy fur
to keep warm in winter?

Who has a huge
body and short,
curved horns?

Who walks a
long way to find
grass to eat?

I do!
I am a bison.

I am also called an
American buffalo. I live in
a big group, called a herd.

Who has big, strong legs for running?

I am the tallest bird in
the world. I cannot fly,
but I can run faster than you!

I do!

I am an ostrich.

Who chirps and sings?

# I do!
I am a grasshopper.

I sing by rubbing my legs against my wings. You'll hear me even if you can't see me!

Who peers above the treetops?

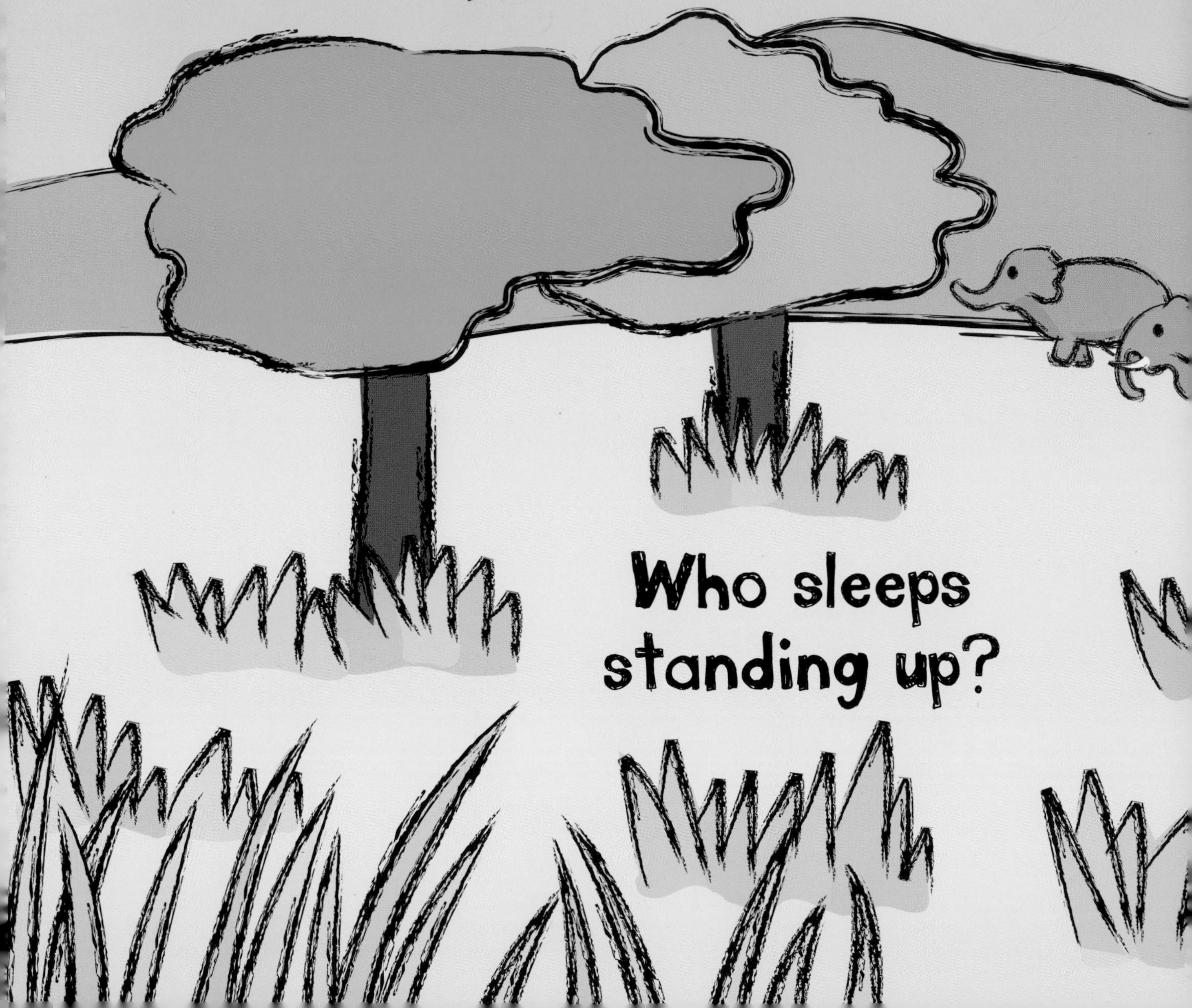

Who sleeps standing up?

Who has a
long, black
tongue?

I am the tallest animal in the world. I can reach the very highest leaves.

I do!
I am a giraffe.

Who has a heavy body and short legs?

Who wallows in mud to keep cool?

Who has a huge
mouth and big,
scary teeth?

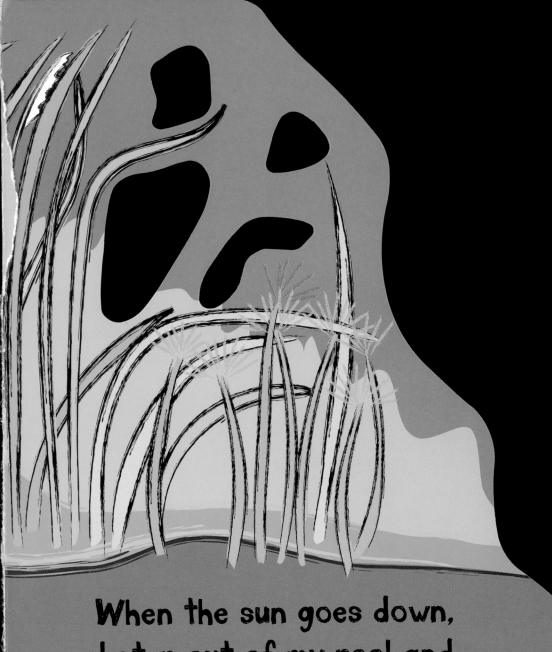

When the sun goes down,
I step out of my pool and
munch on the grass.

I do!
I am a hippopotamus.

# Talking points

1. The first time you read the book together, encourage your child to guess the identity of each animal before turning the flap. Talk together about how they guessed the animal's identity. Did they look at the picture, listen to the words, or use both sets of clues?

2. Ask your child to think about where they live. Use an atlas or a globe to pinpoint your home on the planet. The zebra, tortoise, ostrich, giraffe and hippopotamus in this book all live in Africa. Can you find their home on the planet?

3. A habitat is a place where plants and animals live side by side. An animal's habitat provides all of the food, water and shelter that it needs. Pick an animal together and talk about all the things that animal needs to live.

4. What grassy habitats are there near where you live? Talk about the animals you might see there.